"COME ON, GANG!

WE'RE HAVING
A WARGAME !

The Next World Order Manifesto

by Scott Zagoria

3

Table of Contents

4

PREFACE

The designs outlined in the following pages will -- in all likelihood -- not come to fruition in the very near future since the success of this 'para-system' will/would in fact require an inordinate degree of selfless goodwill and cooperation, specifically on the parts of the most prestigious social classes. Were a comprehensive and morally innovative global platform to be effected, however, these perceptions could well evolve into something more palatable for the majority of the populace.

Be that as it may, the steps proposed in the following pages provide a *hybrid* model for an alternative and hopefully improved social order. The envisioned *system* in fact would rely extensively upon a universal recognition of its perceived merits as an innovative model for personal, inter-personal and inter-species social evolution with the ultimate aim being nothing less than a cohesive and transparent effort to manifest and sustain increasing adherence to the tenets of global justice. It has been suggested that the capitalist impositions inherent in the

'New World Order' are becoming irrelevant as suggested by current developments in Asia and South America.

Meanwhile, environmental threats have emerged as unassailable realities. These results implicate the errant course run by systemic human avarice, as well as the *systemic endorsement* of counter-productive activities by governments struggling to compete. These situational constructs are fueled by malicious attitudes towards other creatures on the planet Earth, which has repercussions for human social interaction.

It might be suggested that the conception of 'original sin', which is shared in some form by many global cultures, could be applied to the consumption of meat by young children. From this act of symbolic cruelty, along with religious proscriptions endorsing the unneeded carnage, multiple inapt perceptions and evils within our social structure become manifest. These conclusions may appear simplistic unless the reader permits him or herself a potentially unfeasible degree of objectivity. Hence, for those who *might* perhaps prefer to engage these fundamental issues more succinctly, I would propose the following.

IN THE HOPE OF POSTPONING THE EXTINCTION OF OUR PLANET'S REMAINING LIFE FORMS, IT IS RECOMMENDED THAT:

A. National Boundaries:
All non-physical boundaries currently acknowledged as existing between globally adjacent populations should be dissolved and/or relegated to historical obscurity without further procrastination. National borders in all instances should be regarded as administrative regions within a planetary infrastructure. Divisive political institutions, including fundamentalist cultural and/or religious political *entities*, as well as transnational militant and coercive commercial affiliations must be dissipated through a revision of those current conditions that engender perceived dominance and hierarchy determined by ethnicity or species..

B. Ecological Directives:
All commercial pollution-producing operations, i.e., industrial and toxic dumps, mining, river damming and diversion, petroleum and natural gas drilling, geothermal exploration, weapons

testing, and other human practices that are generally recognized as having deleterious ecological impact on a local and/or global scale should cease these operations *immediately.* Industry-driven speculation, pseudo-science and prevaricative deliberation can safely be regarded as intended solely to offset or preclude the requisite resuscitative and/or restorative efforts.

C. Political Decision-making, the Legislature and Judicial Apparatus:

Issues of global importance should be acted upon through a remote, regionally-dispersed administration. Both governmental operations and popular participation would largely be rendered via transparent and redundant electronic channels.

Composition of the *administration* would be ethnically 'randomized' through electronic means in order to eliminate preexisting racial and/or class domination; i.e., election to a position of leadership would occur biennially under "blind" electronic conditions with the selected leaders chosen from an eligibility pool (i.e., any global citizen who enters his/her name as eligible, willing, and interested in any position of governance) via random, secure, transparent and verifiable electronic facilitation.

Interference with the formulation of these administrators' political strategies would continue to persist, however the absence of funded lobbyists is a helpful conception. (The recurrent electronic voting irregularities in the U.S. notwithstanding, an imminent development of such a system as described above seems feasible within the theoretical framework being constructed.)

As such, these members of the leadership would serve without permanent membership and only with consultative authority. Re-election would not be permissible, however those deemed worthy of merit would achieve merit and public influence, which should be regarded as sufficient benefits for useful social service. The salary of leadership positions would moreover be of a 'token' nature without implied opportunities for further advancement. As envisioned, any world citizen above the voting age of 18 years would stand equal chance of selection thereby systematically mitigating the antithetical global leadership structure that has prevailed in an essentially unaltered form since ancient times.

Several *million* delegates would be selected to the administration since a large pool of leadership will best ensure statistical mutuality and inherent validity within the electoral and governmental process. Regional discussions and voting procedures might similarly be accomplished via electronic means with the obvious precondition of universal global access. In other words, the bridging of the so-called digital divide remains a preeminent priority. Delegates would continue to live and work in their home communities, convening regularly at quarterly intervals through the electronic administration so as to preserve and enhance direct association with their local constituencies.

Local conditions, on the other hand, seem best regulated at the community level through the coordination of citizens publicly advocating in favor of the best interests of ALL of their assigned neighborhoods' inhabitants. So as to avoid the historical dangers of power abuse, civic committees might evolve as social monitors chosen directly by more traditional village assemblies by which means local concerns could be most appropriately elaborated.

The administrative classifications relevant to the functioning of the 'electronic' leadership need not directly correspond with the socially-oriented local monitors; the latter would retain principal interest in maintaining cultural development and educational parameters, i.e., self-determination and increased self-sufficiency within local communities. When deemed necessary -- as in the case of a significantly divided local electorate -- the community leadership might be similarly chosen by "blind" electronic means. However, these and other local procedural determinations would best be based upon traditional local precedents, whenever feasible. It should be emphasized that matters of disagreement can often be precluded at the local level if responsible social re-adaptation addresses longstanding inequities.

Disagreements and/or divisive issues might, for example, be settled via informed procedural compromise, i.e., perhaps a virtual world interface protocol appropriate for supportive, definitive, and collaborative decision-making. This uniform system of electronic negotiation might be instituted globally, while these proscriptions would further serve to augment traditional self-determination and local arbitration methods if applied in conjunction with on-site or remote non-binding intervention implemented by skilled and mutually disinterested mediators.

In their current form, judicial systems worldwide essentially serve to promulgate the authority of the local, privileged oligarchy. With the movement towards elimination of global class distinctions there will likely come a corresponding decrease in the incidence of crime and dissatisfaction. The remnant political conceptualizations of communism, state socialism and capitalism have in a sense become inherently obsolete. The present *neo-corporate* conditions reiterate prior constructs that were enunciated by Polybius around 180 BC, i.e., the cycle of anacyclosis. As he noted, any prevailing global system engenders the seeds of its own destruction. However, it might equally be suggested that all prior systems relied upon social and material inequity, while the current phase of neo-corporatism merely offers a refinement upon the conventional oligarchic approach to micro-management of global resources.

All resistance has come to be regarded as insurgence or intransigence, both of which run contrary to the functions of the commercial/military corpocracy and its assigned protectorate, the judiciary. The 'law' has been largely discredited globally since it currently applies to the preservation of cultural class prestige at the expense of the more salient function of the judiciary, i.e., to enhance the potential for benign cooperative development beyond the functions of expediency and the cloak of officiousness that largely preempt popular revision of societal (i.e., situationally-contrived and/or defined) structures and relationships.

Legislative and judiciary functions will increasingly concern themselves with the equitable distribution of communal material and resources. The cross-cultural and multi-class composition of these evolving supervising entities will additionally promote increased logic, beneficence and common sense in opposition to unbridled ambition for wealth and prestige. Issues relating to property redistribution, environmental protection, land usage and the coordination of social welfare programs might fall increasingly under the domain of judicial assemblies since criminal cases will decrease in parallel with the implementation of judicious policies, educational enhancements and cultural revivification.

D. *Police and Military Dissipation:*

Concurrent with the dissolution of non-topographic frontiers, all military, paramilitary and police units worldwide would best be reorganized and/or disbanded, whenever feasible. All weaponry, ballistic ordnance, materiel, heavy explosives, timing and detonating devices, as well as chemical, genetic, and biological weapons (in addition to all technology pertaining thereto) should be destroyed in a timely manner at *acceptable* destruction sites (as determined by scientific committees).

Metal, plastic, alloy and new material research and production should in the future be engineered and intended for non-ballistic and non-military use while conforming to strict ecological directives. To this end, those with extensive technological capabilities must not participate in any manner towards future weapons production or research; every effort must also be made to preclude the incentives for any individual to act contrary to these norms. The motivation for transfer of weapons-related technical data should likewise be undermined by removing financial and global espionage incentives, which will hopefully be a significantly beneficial characteristic of global disarmament in concord with a globally resolute orientation towards uniform removal of oppressive social organs. Compliance must be both voluntary and mandatory in both policy and practice to ensure that all weapons with the potential for causing destruction not be allowed to fall into the "wrong" hands by eliminating the dangerous and presumptuous notion that there can possibly exist any "right" ones.

Private, corporate or cooperative possession of any weapon (with a firing mechanism or otherwise) is misguided. Sporting weapons, as well as those for personal, home or business security are similarly inappropriate. Knives, swords, spears and other purportedly "decorative" weapons could be considered on individual bases after their potential for causing harm has been removed (i.e., dulled blades, soldered firing mechanisms, etc.). In general, all implements intended to harm any complex animal life should by way of 'human decency' be unconditionally removed from the social sphere.

Articles such as matches and rope which are clearly not manufactured primarily for belligerent purposes can ultimately be regarded as intrinsically safe only within the context of a non-aggressive societal structure, while it seems unlikely that the same argument could be made in regards to firearms or weapons of mass destruction. Discussions regarding per capita gun ownership in Canada and Switzerland notwithstanding, the populations of these two nations would likely be at the forefront of any effort to conform to global armistice since their ultimate national objectives are purportedly peaceful in spite of hunting and armed neutrality traditions.

With the disbanding of traditional police, national guard, state guard and internal/government security forces, unarmed and well-organized community safety groups could be formed in their stead to assist during natural emergencies, rescue operations, civic projects, etc. With worldwide military resources freed up and made available for more productive community-support programs, "security" might cease to be manifested as repression.

E.   Land Ownership:
The ownership of dormant and/or vacant private and corporate land holdings should be addressed such that the perpetuity of medieval territorial dominance by overweening entities might ultimately become an anachronism.   Authorized access and use of unoccupied land might, for instance, devolve to future land tenants for the duration of such tenure thereby superseding prior ownership claims.   A system of procedural compromise might be obligatory in any resultant disagreement, arbitration to be supervised by respected members of the community regulated by common sense, a neutral arbitration protocol and a significant level of cooperation. Private and corporate-owned 'estate' land might similarly be placed under the care of the community which would determine land usage parameters such that large unused tracts adjoining personal or corporate-owned construction could instead be employed for community benefit.

F. Corporate Control:
Preexisting multinational and large local corporate entities must revise their practices in

order to conform to a cooperative world society. In return for the elimination of international commercial tariffs and vastly enlarged consumer markets (for needed goods and services), there may also come a cessation of competitive rancor. Also, through the abandonment of blind profit motives, an increased sense of corporate cooperation would correspond with the elimination of *obsolete* business enterprises including those that are military-related, toxic waste producers, *lowest common denominator* media entities or environmentally/culturally deleterious corporations. In order to function within the global business sphere, entities wishing to operate under alternative parameters would thereby agree to abide by a comprehensive series of reviews. These periodic surveys would examine corporate policy including, but not limited to: employee relations, hiring practices, profit structure, corporate ethics, land-use provisions, management policies, waste removal, community relations, product quality control and financial operations.

It is crucial that corporations be motivated by various incentives and structural redefining to shift from self-serving, professionally sanctioned loyalty to shareholders towards increased arts patronage and community service. The disposal or storage of *black money* through traditional corporate financing means remains one of the most fundamental issues that needs to be confronted in this regard.

G. Monetary Policy:

Concurrent with next world order societal evolution comes irresistibly the disestablishment of monetary currency. This course is the only viable means towards achieving a social organism wherein there can be no more "haves and have-nots", while the present international wealth hierarchy can be confronted via renovating the system at its most basic levels

In this regard, monetary reform is crucial. Although expressed only half-heartedly in the Declaration of Independence, the "right to life, liberty and the pursuit of happiness" is nonetheless noteworthy. Whether one is able to afford to exercise these 'inalienable rights' is, as the saying goes, self-evident. All beings are created equal and all living things have unequivocal rights irregardless of current misconceptions. Profit motive and material gain have never produced worthy enterprises and have traditionally constituted the mechanism whereby colonizing powers are ultimately reduced; nor have these mundane schemes developed in any real sense as crucial motivational forces towards global peace.

On the other hand, envisaging a commodious means of planetary reorganization in recognition of the cataclysms of the future -- and ones that can only serve to oblige changes on a monumental scale-- will require an abandonment of the principal means whereby oppressive social classes have maintained their prominence and ability to divide larger populations by creating scenarios wherein people oppose each other, in effect acting against their own best interests.

Divide and conquer is a function of power brokers; for several thousand years their mandate has been provided by possession of paper money. Until current global inequities are addressed, there will continue to be insufficient food in the world for all living creatures; and not coincidentally, those without food generally have no money. A recognition that promiscuous consumption has preceded the dissolution of every significant historical empire since the Mesolithic era should also be an academic priority.

Rapidly increasing population growth combined with far less rapidly increasing food production suggests the situation is dire. The only sane solution is to feed everyone whether they can pay for it or not while simultaneously increasing available sources and seriously effecting to reduce the global human population.

Perhaps expanded material rewards of unusual artistry or uncommon technical sophistication should be forthcoming to those performing extraordinary service to the populace. Capable educators and administrators, for example, should be brought to the forefront. Therefore, a system of non-monetary reward would best serve and might be instituted to recruit and reward skilled personnel. Basic life necessities, however, should in no way be dependent upon such service: the government represents a social welfare mechanism, and not as an oppressive force.

H. Taxation:

The development of social welfare programs globally should be the principal function of the next order system. The means by which this can be accomplished must be readily available and must be provided for in written legislation. Hence, the transport of provisions across diverse regions, as well as in advance of impending disasters is deemed a critical component of the systemic reformation. Transfer of material and resources from other segments of the world economy (i.e. military, etc.) could provide the impetus for the redirection of needed goods and services strategically warehoused.

Under the present commercial imperatives, vast quantities of non-renewable resources are of course being regularly depleted, while tax reserves are most commonly being funneled into misguided projects (both military and infrastructural) and various corporate holdings, in addition to 'black money' accounts that cannot be traced. As social welfare mechanisms and infrastructure deteriorates, the middle and lower classes are obliged to compete for dwindling access to basic social access. Meanwhile, the wealthiest individuals and companies, as is common knowledge, pay no tax or very little.

Whenever a wealthy businessman, evangelist or white-collar criminal is discovered to have been operating in excess and to the exclusion of the tax system, it is not uncommon for internal revenue agents to be called in and arrests are duly made.   However, it is equally common knowledge that those who are ultimately apprehended usually are placed in alternative prisons that share little in common with the traditional penal system. Upon release, these individuals are generally sufficiently mollified to accommodate more acceptable tax loopholes in the future.   As such, the tax system is principally concerned not with validating the origins of taxpayers' income but more specifically with assurances that covert governmental spending is able to continue unabated. Taxation without representation remains at the heart of systemic corruption.

The following social structures should be implicit elements of the next world global economy, i.e., they should emerge as outcomes of the system's production rather than from workers' wages. These would include alternative energy programs, social welfare organizations, agricultural collectives and information bases, strategic resettlement projects, ecological compatibility centers, education and outreach programs, as well as the requirements for optimal legislative and judicial functions. The traditional solution of turning over the reigns of power to the privileged elite in order to alleviate the suffering of the poor might best be regarded as a failed effort and one that has repeatedly proven futile during 5,000 years of human civilization. It seems incumbent upon the coming generations to establish a different model.

I. Urban Redevelopment:
The resettlement of a substantial percentage of global inner-city dwellers to more congenial, healthful, and non-congested areas is clearly essential if urban decay is to be reversed, as is the elimination of the significantly deleterious effects attributable to automobile and industrial pollution. Land renovation in the form of enlarged park land, innovative architectural

styles, cross-city bicycle and walking paths, intelligent mass transit implementation and urban reforestation and garden projects would be achievable improvements.

Certainly, the issues relating to which individuals or families should be "entitled" to increasingly limited inner-city housing is contentious. One possible solution might be short-term tenancies of six-month duration which would be selected from a digital pool of 'candidates'.

All interested persons (i.e., those listing themselves as eligible) would have equal opportunity of obtaining a limited-term tenancy in renovated urban environs regardless of their nationality, race, occupation, etc. Built-up suburban areas might undergo similar *depopulations* wherever human habitation threatens to overwhelm the natural balance.

J. Rural Migration Policy:
As even wealthy urban inhabitants are discovering, the idea of securing oneself from hostile elements is rapidly becoming a ludicrous

conception. The effects of rampant violence; widespread weapon and hard drug availability; crumbling social infrastructures, buildings and community facilities; brutally institutionalized racism; mis-education of an alarming variety; increasingly ill-trained, badly-informed and well-armed police; the ensuing and imminent spread of contagious diseases (i.e. increased incidences of tuberculosis, cholera, typhus, AIDS, swine flue, etc.) due largely to diminishing sanitation, health care, overcrowding and inadequate urban planning; mismanagement ensconced within the very marrow of the political framework; debilitating automobile and industrial pollution; increasing stress resultant from man-made noise pollution; drinking water contamination, outdated treatment techniques and over-chlorination; lead pipe erosion, asbestos poisoning and acid rain; airborne chemical pollution; oil barge and refinery spills into public waterways; and the increasing separation of the urban populace from healthful contact with nature offer a partial representation of the highly volatile conditions being created across the planet in the majority of large cities. The solution lies partially in the sensible resettlement of city dwellers and their families, as well as the introduction of various practicable incentives to resuscitate deforested, derelict and marginal land where various work projects (i.e. reforestation, agriculture, etc.) might be implemented through direct community action. Sensitivity to local ecologies and a serious commitment on the part of the human species to significantly curtail global population growth are imperative to the success of resettlement.

K. Mass Transportation and the Elimination of Personal Internal-combustion Vehicles:

Private and commercial uses of gasoline powered vehicles should be replaced by cleaner, quieter forms of transportation. Diesel engine trucks for personal usage should be immediately banned. Battery powered vehicles which achieve speeds in excess of 100 m.p.h. on a 300 mile charge are already being designed; certainly the infrastructural requirements for hybrid and/or electric vehicles remain of paramount importance. Graduate level university projects should be introduced globally with any and all feasible conceptions being developed with an eye towards approaching 0% emissions.

The continued presence of commercial vehicles specifically in urban environs should correspond with the necessity of the services they perform. In general, private and commercial vehicles (as well as government and community-owned vehicles) should be vastly reduced in number, or excluded completely whenever feasible, especially within heavily populated city districts.

No Sacrifice Is too Great

for Low, Low Prices!

In any case, limited vehicle use (of improved design) might be made available for citizens more in accordance with their needs than their means. Guidelines for vehicle usage would be determined by community leadership rather than federal mandates. Eventually personal vehicles would cease to be regarded as the building blocks of status, but rather as the means whereby critical emergency and social service vehicles might be made quickly available to all citizens when required.

Furthermore, mass transit alternatives should be explored and instituted unilaterally to replace private automobiles. Slide, rail, gravity, and other transport designs can in many instances replace outdated underground and surface systems providing for more innovative usage of raised-ground level platforms that might serve to assist the significant majority of urban inhabitants. Intercity, suburban, rural and mountainous areas might similarly be traversed by mass transit networks replacing auto traffic to a large degree.

For instance, instead of a heavily used road

traversing a hilly suburban neighborhood, a system of controlled transport might be developed to operate on a track mechanism which could be summoned electronically to pick up a caller near his/her home in order to transfer them to an adjoining "major road", i.e., a mass transport intersection. Such a system could ultimately (especially within the framework of 1 billion new Chinese vehicles) provide faster access than automobiles with only slightly less convenience. Additionally, noise and air pollution would be markedly decreased, automobile traffic would cease to be a major problem, and thousands of lives would be saved annually from accidents and the unhealthy effects of constant confinement in automobiles, generally at the expense of walking and related exercise.

Extensive natural preserves, new parkland, long-distance hiking and bicycle trails, recreation facilities and community-responsive theaters, galleries and buildings would hopefully augment the revised landscape.

L. Social Welfare End Resettlement Policy:

All complex living animals are equally deserving of access to sufficient food, shelter, medical care/immunization and other necessities. Means should be investigated assiduously such that starvation and other existing global inequities will be rectified across the spectrum of human and other animal life. It is the obligation of any civilized system to attempt to raise the standard of life for all inhabitants thereof, especially those in direst need. Information concerning impending natural disasters (i.e. earthquakes, rising water, high winds, etc.) should be widely disseminated, while emergency and evacuation should of course be advanced, as should be the mechanisms to provide emergency relief anywhere promptly and without interference.

Worldwide data networks could be established in order to record land tenancy data, providing global access to available land not already protected against development which could thereupon be settled by any world citizen (assuming all land use proscriptions are being adhered to). Reclaimed land, former wilderness, previously barren soil, etc. can then be strategically settled with an emphasis upon causing minimal damage to the ecosystem. Respect for nature and the ability to coexist harmoniously with it are prerequisites for this effort.

These data banks should also maintain records of available food and material surpluses existing within neighboring areas to permit essential relief under emergency conditions. Provision for the wide scale transport required for the envisioned global resettlement need not be particularly daunting with respect to systems already in operation. Aircraft and cargo ships currently used for troop movements, military craft currently employed for the transfer of material and ordnance, and other available transport would be scaled down and then redeployed for civilian resettlement after being upgraded with more viable engine designs whenever feasible. Improvements in locally-produced food, shelter and energy combined with an enhanced availability of technology supported through comprehensive educational de-standardization would offer hope for sensible development and eventual self-sufficiency amongst currently impoverished classes of the global community.

M. Prohibitions Against Violence Towards Complex Animal Life:

Repeating cycles of violence pose the fundamental block to planetary progress. For many reasons it should be impermissible to: (a) destroy any complex [anything with a face?] living animal for food consumption or industrial purposes (except, as regards food consumption, under hardship conditions under which taboos against cannibalism would be similarly devalued), (b) make use of any complex animal for scientific and/or research purposes, (c) hunt or fish (except insofar as no firearms are introduced and no animals are killed or seriously endangered, i.e., strictly for sport without barbs, pointed hooks or live ammunition in the hope that these practices might soon be viewed as 'pointless'), or (d) restrict unnaturally (i.e. solely in cages or other unusual confinement) or in any way cause misery to any domesticated or normally wild animal. Land and resources used for animal slaughter should be returned to more productive and less destructive uses.

Vegetarianism should predominate among all species to the greatest extent possible. Among humans it would hopefully come to be both voluntary and mandatory in correspondence with an evolving presence as planetary benefactor.

The horror of animal slaughter has been deeply suppressed throughout most human populations since the most recent ice age when vegetation was scarce. New climatic conditions require reconditioning and animal slaughter should cease. A concerted effort might be made to gradually (re)introduce omnivorousness or, preferably, vegetarianism into carnivorous wild animal populations. (It is interesting to note, for instance, that one of humanity's most ancient insect enemies, the mosquito, lives primarily on fruits and vegetables rather than blood.) Although the concept seems irrational to our understanding of biological systems, the long-term implications for planetary peace remain a matter of an extension of evolutionary principles to cognitive functions, as opposed to physical characteristics alone. Physical features such as carnivorous animal behavior are results of preconditioned environmental attributes; this equation can be readily reversed during the course of several centuries (or, perhaps several decades if due recognition is addressed to these developments and conditions), i.e., psychic evolution.

N. Reforestation Program:

Worldwide reforestation and the reintroduction of depleted indigenous vegetation should become the principal occupation of millions. The remaining large, undisturbed watershed, woodlands and rain-forests would best be set aside and preserved. Any further destruction of rain-forest, in particular, is clearly misguided as is wholesale deforestation for geothermal exploitation, wood/paper production or human habitation.

It is to be hoped that careful planning might eventually permit whole bio-systems to be restored to vitality. Moreover, reforestation and wide-scale production of rapid growing annual vegetation (such as hemp) are crucial to any 'greenhouse effect' reversal effort.

O. Cannabis Production:

Great tracts of land should be set aside for, and millions employed in, the production of cannabis and cannabis-related industries. Some strains may be grown for seed, others for biomass and some for sensimilla flowers. Cannabis seed contains very high protein concentrations while hemp stalks provide excellent sources for building material, rope, clothing, methanol and biomass energy. The flowers have wide-ranging and documented medicinal value.

Although cannabis (marijuana) is illegal it offers perhaps the only hope both industrially and psychologically for the survival of our planet. The ability of cannabis to withstand relatively harsh conditions and to grow in almost all climates, as well as its being the fastest growing, annually renewable food and energy source in the world is sufficient reason for rapid and well-supported cannabis production on a global scale. Moreover, cannabis releases no poisonous sulfur compounds when combusted (as do oil, coal, etc.) and the growing plant's CO_2 intake balances its CO_2 output when burned. Thus, when applied in conjunction with reforestation, increased agricultural production and sharply decreased fossil fuel and other industrial pollution one could expect the gradual cessation and subsequent reversal of the "greenhouse effect" which is one of the most cataclysmic and imminent dangers we face. Perhaps equally important is the realization that cannabis could mean the end of world starvation, homelessness, fuel shortages and substantial physical and psychological ills.

P. Alternate Energy Policy:
There should be rapid increases in development of alternative energy forms including: wind farms, solar, co-generation, natural gas and, especially, hemp grown for biomass and methanol production. Newly developed energy innovation of promising nature should be promoted (not suppressed by "Big Business" interests) such that community-based energy programs may be instituted globally. Petroleum, nuclear, coal and other polluting and/or nonrenewable energy sources should be phased out as rapidly and to whatever degree possible. Misguided energy projects such as geothermal and river diversion should be reconsidered if

found to be ecologically unsound.

Q. Nuclear Facility Conversion and Waste Policy:

Waste from, and processes employed by nuclear and chemical industries are of critical concern, especially since their toxicity may last many thousands of years. It is not inconceivable in this regard that distant generations may experience devastating radioactive storms, water contamination and shortages, mass epidemics and repeated reproductive mutations through the continuing abuses of our own military and industrial complexes. For example, ground water seepage of spent radioactive material near the Savannah, Georgia nuclear weapons facility produced mutated turtles several miles away.

In addition, frequent accidental and intentional ocean discharges of radioactive waste, repeated "mishandling" of deployed nuclear weapons, the meltdowns at Chernobyl and Three Mile Island, the deaths of many thousands in Bhopal, India from a Union Carbide chemical blunder and the appalling and undiminished toxification of global drinking water supplies do not portend well for the future of hazardous industrial substances and their disposal. The global science community should begin to address these issues in serious and practical fashion. Moreover, the means to determine realistic and sensible methods of clean-up and "disposal" as well as the whereabouts of illegally dumped nuclear waste should be investigated fully.

In the present environment of unscrupulous and foolish business practice, nuclear waste is not only dumped into the sea but also buried in landfill or sold to removal services which leave it piled in Third World deserts (as some multinationals presently do in Sonora, Mexico and elsewhere). As one of the most serious problems facing the planet today (and forever),cynical legalistic viewpoints must be swept away and a positive outlook restored regarding the future.

R. Household Garbage Policy:
Only fully biodegradable and/or recyclable materials should be used for household and business packaging worldwide. Corporate and consumer waste "habits", especially in the

wealthier nations, must decrease significantly and better means of disposal, treatment and recycling found. Existing dump-sites should eventually be dissipated [landfill?] and these areas restored to nature.

S. Media Issues:
Electronic media should be the domain of the artist and the educator. Commercial values placed on creative work are unavoidably detrimental. Advertisers and military recruitment agencies would best remain uninvolved with sponsorship. Television, radio and film (especially with the advent of satellite transmission) have emerged as primary tools with unmatched potential to break down class`and cultural barriers. For example, unilateral access to video/sound recording equipment and instruction would provide a wealth of interesting, educational and sophisticated material in comparison to the closed multi-billion dollar "entertainment" industry which is responsible, along with its sponsors, for the current rash of propaganda news, authoritarian violence, Sunday golf, "real life" soap operas and sit-coms and the ever-

popular game shows. The commercialization of film, theater and the broadcast media is, in short, a lowest common denominator sedative and an abuse of power. Support for independent creative work should increase substantially and be offered solely on basis of merit (i.e. with artists' proposals considered on "blind" bases to eliminate arts administration cronyism).

Increased access to broadcast frequencies should be forthcoming permitting new and interesting work to be presented uncensored and undubbed. In time, depictions of gratuitous violence and glorification of civil brutality can be expected to diminish as societal ignorance and systemic abuses undergo corresponding reductions.

T. Revised Education Policies:
Parents should take greater responsibility for their children's development and, therefore, would be best served to pay heed to their own educations. In this regard, global educational policy might be revised as follows: (1) All children and adults should have access to educational facilities and instructional materials; (2) school curriculum should be determined for

the most part locally with the language and culture of the home region emphasized; and (3) a global core curriculum should also be developed and presented in schools and learning materials unilaterally. This core curriculum would hopefully impart a respect for all life, commitment towards mutual growth and communication across cultural barriers, increased geographical awareness and, perhaps, education in a new and improved fashion.

The basic educational objective is 100% literacy among the world's adult population and increased global sensitivity with enhanced cross-cultural awareness. For this purpose, readily available community equipment and materials should be made available, especially where no schools, as such exist. Broad educational exchanges need be established in order to encourage creative and multi-cultural experimentation. The potential dangers inherent in the creation of a cross-cultural core curriculum are substantial.

It is crucial that such a program not be envisioned as a way to make people more alike, but on the contrary should bolster the survival of indigenous and ancient cultural elements. To avoid subversion or manipulation, any core curriculum must endeavor to be bias-free in every respect. World history, for example, should present clear and comprehensible depictions of opposing views, the underlying theme being the preference of global cooperation as compared to global confrontation.

U. Alternate Food Sources:

Soy, kelp, grains and cannabis seed are very promising food sources which along with expanded fruit and vegetable production offer hope for escape from the cycle of planetary starvation for man and beast. The ability of cannabis plants so bred to produce seed, for instance, is astounding and wide scale planting could alleviate great suffering. The only problem is simply this: For not very good reasons cannabis is illegal in nearly every country.

If the reader requires further information on the utility of cannabis seed as a food source or the circumstances surrounding the "not very good reasons" which have led to marijuana criminalization worldwide, please see 19th Century Medical Cannabis. (Createspace, 2015) Increased ecological sensitivity and the availability of previously unsettleable (as well as formerly meat-producing) land would dramatically increase fruit and vegetable yields worldwide. As previously mentioned, emergency airlift services might be coordinated so as to be available where and when required to offer aid to those in greatest need. Further advances might stem from agricultural collectives, shifts in land use,information dissemination, adjustments in, water policy and improvements in water transportation to dry farmland. For further reading on alternate food sources and land usage, see John Robbins' Diet for a New Planet.

V. Family Policy and Zero Population Growth: A significant aspect of the educational effort and public service organizational outlook will pertain to focusing awareness on the need to slow birthrates among the human population. Cultural biases in favor of large families must be adjusted, as must available services for unwanted and un-provided for children. Much improved social welfare mechanisms are critical in order that impoverished populations no longer require large extended families to ensure their well-being. Similarly, a new social welfare system should evolve providing continuing support and useful education for any individuals that so request. Fundamentalist religious influence which undermines zero growth efforts should be dissipated by making the world populace aware of the serious dangers of overpopulation. In this regard, improved contraceptive design, perhaps in the form of a testosterone suppressor, is a high scientific priority. Dissemination of available contraceptives should proceed rapidly and on global scale.

Abortion should be generally discouraged but unilaterally available. Unwanting mothers might be requested to provide good pre-natal care until birth at which time the infants could be placed with loving families.

W. Domestic Animal Policy:

Increased dog/cat ownership should be strongly encouraged. Dogs should be trained for companionship or for work, rather-than attack protection. Dog-fighting for money (an unfortunately wide scale and barbarous practice) must be stopped. Vicious dog laws which are in place would best be strengthened with dog owners bearing the brunt of legal responsibility. (The banning of specific breeds [i.e. pit bulls] is wrong.) Moreover, leash laws might be relaxed in most instances and maximum freedom of movement offered to non-threatening pets.

The practice of euthanizing un-owned dogs, cats, horses and other domesticated animals should cease. Animal welfare organizations can be reorganized, their sole function being the collection of endangered stray animals and transportation of such to regional facilities located in enclosed rural areas. Shelter and food would be provided on these large tracts. The model envisioned would include 20 or 30 well-distanced, prefabricated structures provided with water, heat (if required), old furniture and substantial attached woodland to each dwelling.

Well-trained personnel would be provided as required. Animals would be gradually socialized, if necessary, to promote harmonious relations among the great majority of dogs/cats. School children and others from inner-city areas could visit these separate canine and feline settlements perhaps discovering the friendship of dogs and cats for the first time.

This kind of rural education could be part of the deurbanization process by increasing sensitivity to issues of ecological and ethical importance while providing healthy exposure to more nature-oriented lifestyles. Perceived financial drawbacks to such a non-euthanasia policy are far outweighed by ethical considerations. In any case, the elimination of long-term cage confinement, euthanization facilities and related human staff in addition to savings derived through the regional centralization of existing dog/cat "welfare" organizations make. The proposed transformation of these facilities is more attractive. Moreover, it is not unlikely that some commercial applications might be found in these settlements and that in time they might come to support themselves to some degree.

X. Religious/Social Freedoms:

Universal freedoms clearly should be guaranteed although unwarranted privileges (such as large Church holdings and the overabundance of racist and class-ist private golf courses/private clubs) would best be reversed in favor of community use. Policy should be guided by the increased need for cross-cultural contact and mutual appreciation instead of striation and ignorant sectarianism. Fundamentalists must relax their disparate viewpoints to embrace the tapestry of religious divergence. Social freedoms should include proscriptions against prosecution for victimless crimes.

These reactionary legal dealings undermine the law's authority and promote belligerent and wrongful police usage. Moreover, no one should be imprisoned for drug use or possession and those presently incarcerated should be released and restituted.

Concurrent with global societal reorganization and unilateral availability of cannabis, honest drug education might combine with more humane attitudes towards addiction to engender a substantial decrease in the numbers and degree of anti-sociality among hard drug users. Furthermore, it follows that cigarette and alcohol promotion as well as pharmaceutical drug prescription should be curtailed in favor of alternative cures of less self-destructive nature.

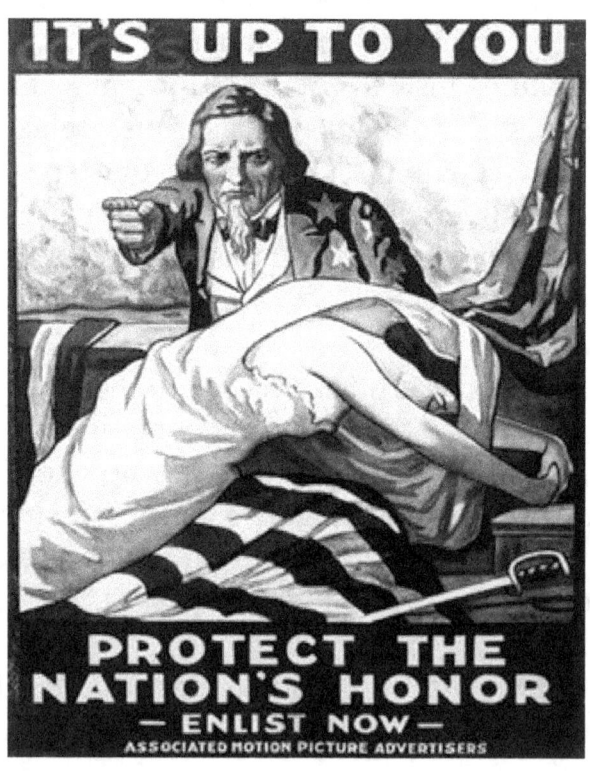

Y. Water Policy:

As existing water supplies become increasingly contaminated, fresh drinking water will become a highly salable commodity perhaps eclipsing precious metals in value. Global warming can be expected to speed up desertification and melt polar ice caps/fresh water glaciers, causing large scale coastal flooding, water shortages and climatic variations. Ocean desalinization plants may eventually become the principal source for fresh water.   Substantial drinking water costs to consumers and businesses threaten a marked upswing in multinational control with the further erosion of personal freedom worldwide. A sensible global water policy and the concurrent reversal of global warming trends suggest a viable alternative to this ensuing doomsday vision.

Along with clean air and uncontaminated soil, fresh water is a fundamental right of all living creatures and one well worth protection with decreases in urban population and abandonment of livestock breeding (most agricultural water is used in livestock production) may come an easing of the problem. As mentioned elsewhere, advances in irrigation and water transportation may also help, as will population decreases, resettlement and measures designed to preserve remaining topsoil from erosion.

Z. Employment Issues:

All repetitive and/or dangerous work should continue towards total mechanization; global elimination of human exploitation in the workplace, as in other places, being the objective. With food and basic comforts guaranteed, it is true that motivation to have a "job" may diminish, though there will always be a substantial segment of the populace which gravitates towards physical labor. Those who prefer to employ large portions of their time in diligent pursuits such as self-education, physical improvement, meditation, personal analysis or creative endeavor (i.e. those presently considered lazy) should be equally tolerated.

It is becoming a bittersweet reality that unlike previous eras, we finally have the means to provide basic living necessities for all people (and animals). Our current crisis continues to be the result of corrupt, cynical leadership which resists the requisite systemic alterations to further their own interests. Many civilized nations already recognize welfare provision as a principal responsibility of their systems; moreover, one of indisputably beneficial character to the community.

Anyone doubting the sagacity of these attitudes might schedule a short, informative tour of New York City, which has adopted no such "welfare" stance. A further result of corporate and governmental systemic conspiracy is the propagation of two abhorrent tenets. The first, already discussed, concerns mutually congratulatory tax loopholes extended to wealthy individuals and businesses. The second is the widespread work "ethic" that postulates hard work and high pay inversely, such that wealthy "workers" do the least. Naturally, they are paid more because their "responsibility" is greater. This responsibility extends, too, into the environmental, social, political and psychological realm in which we live.

Be that as it may, additional incentives could be devised to encourage physical participation in global work projects and to promote technical, medical and white-collar training (of administrative skills particularly) for those interested in public service (i.e. not those whose overriding "interest" is personal advantage).

Nevertheless, one's choice of vocation should in no way affect one's right to basic necessities.

It is unseemly that any being be deemed more worthy of sustenance than another. An expanded range of lifestyles and work activities would be desirable. For instance, an extended family (or collective) might live and work a 20-acre plot of land growing vegetables and cannabis flowers for personal consumption and barter. Available store or home-delivered goods would supplement this "income".

On an individual might choose to work on any of the various worldwide projects such as hemp/produce farming, reforestation, urban redevelopment, new settlement construction and services, transportation services and construction, domestic animal settlements, outreach educational/medical services, scientific/archaeological projects, land reclamation service, wildlife preservation, parks management, social services, childcare, etc.

EPILOGUE
Cooperation vs. Competition:

Competition is the practice of exploiting one's advantage over another and the course whereby the "enemy" can most readily be vanquished. Exploitation is closely related to submissiveness.

The notion of aggressive competition as a positive factor in social evolution is fallacious, although it is often invoked to help explain away existing societal inequities. This serves in part to promulgate the psychological/physical brutality required for forcing unflinching submission to privileged authority and the corresponding cold-blooded survival instinct necessary to subdue unprotected populations.

Nationalism, religion, language, race, sex and species-ism have been intoned since time immemorial to draw hierarchical distinctions between populations promoting thereby the interests of one segment over another. The reasoning which proclaims that competition is essential to progress is part and parcel of the myth. The industrial "successes" of capitalist nations are frequently cited. It currently appears, for instance, that Western capitalism has overwhelmed so-called communist systems. Unfortunately, the enlargement of police/military structures to unassailable proportions and the sequestration of available resources at the expense of the public-sector follow. However, when the non-renewable resources fail and basic necessities are no longer available to large populations, one should not be surprised to discover that the competitive instinct may transmogrify into martial law while mercenaries abound. The interrelationship of competition, authority and privileged wealth is systemic and must be addressed succinctly for it is at the core of the continuing global destruction and the increasingly callous gaps between wealth and poverty.

Meanwhile, the perfidy of the present global leadership (with few notable exceptions) fervently reiterates the ubiquitous interests of privileged members of the global populace. Yet those issues relevant to any discussion of the means whereby morally corrupt authoritarians ascend (or are erected upon) the ladder of political ascendancy resides beyond the scope of the present discussion. These models of wealth oppressing poverty have persisted under the vast majority of historical leadership systems, and unless systemic realities are confronted as they pertain to planet Earth in the opening decades of the new millennium, these systemic inequities will likely disrupt human habitation on this planet.

As of June 28, 2008, the human population approximates 6,704,845,726 globally (statistics from worldometers.info).   "Though accounting for only 5 percent of the world's population, Americans consume 26 percent of the world's energy." (American Almanac) There need be little discussion at this late point in time to discern whether our system is out of control.

-fin-

[Author's Note: This text was begun in 1997 and has been published for the first time in 2015.]

www.ingramcontent.com/pod-product-compliance
Lightning Source LLC
Chambersburg PA
CBHW060646290526
45793CB00001B/421